Native Americans

The Pawnee

Barbara A. Gray-Kanatiiosh

ABDO Publishing Company

visit us at
www.abdopublishing.com

Published by ABDO Publishing Company, 8000 West 78th Street, Edina, Minnesota 55439. Copyright © 2002 by Abdo Consulting Group, Inc. International copyrights reserved in all countries. No part of this book may be reproduced in any form without written permission from the publisher.

Printed in the United States of America, North Mankato, Minnesota.
012002 102012

Illustrations: David Kanietakeron Fadden
Interior Photos: Corbis, AP/Wide World
Editors: Bob Italia, Tamara L. Britton, Kate A. Furlong, Kristin Van Cleaf
Book Design & Graphics: Neil Klinepier

Library of Congress Cataloging-in-Publication Data

Gray-Kanatiiosh, Barbara A., 1963-
   The Pawnee / Barbara A. Gray-Kanatiiosh.
     p. cm. -- (Native Americans)
  Includes index.
  Summary: An introduction to the history, social life and customs, and present life of the Pawnee Indians.
  ISBN 1-57765-607-5
  1. Pawnee Indians--Juvenile literature. [1. Pawnee Indians. 2. Indians of North America--Great Plains.] I. Title. II. Native Americans (Edina, Minn.)

E99.P3 G74 2002
978.004'979--dc21

2001055277

About the Author: Barbara Gray-Kanatiiosh, JD

Barbara Gray-Kanatiiosh, JD, is an Akwesasne Mohawk. She has a Juris Doctorate from Arizona State University, where she was one of the first recipients of ASU's special certificate in Indian Law. She is currently pursuing a Ph.D. in Justice Studies at ASU and is focusing on Native American issues. Barbara works hard to educate children about Native Americans through her writing and Web site where children may ask questions and receive a written response about the Haudenosaunee culture. The Web site is: www.peace4turtleisland.org

Illustrator: David Kanietakeron Fadden

David Kanietakeron Fadden is a member of the Akwesasne Mohawk Wolf Clan. His work has appeared in publications such as *Akwesasne Notes, Indian Time*, and the *Northeast Indian Quarterly*. Examples of his work have also appeared in various publications of the Six Nations Indian Museum in Onchiota, NY. His work has also appeared in "How The West Was Lost: Always The Enemy," produced by Gannett Production, which appeared on the Discovery Channel. David's work has been exhibited in Albany, NY; the Lake Placid Center for the Arts; Centre Strathearn in Montreal, Quebec; North Country Community College in Saranac Lake, NY; Paul Smith's College in Paul Smiths, NY; and at the Unison Arts & Learning Center in New Paltz, NY.

Contents

Where They Lived 4
Society 6
Food 8
Homes 10
Clothing 12
Crafts 14
Family 16
Children 18
Myths 20
War 22
Contact with Europeans 24
Crooked Hand 26
The Pawnee Today 28
Glossary 31
Web Sites 31
Index 32

Where They Lived

The Pawnee (paw-NEE) Nation was made up of four **bands**. The bands were called the Skidi, Chaui, Kitkihahki, and Petahauirata. They spoke Pawnee, a language in the Caddoan language family.

The Pawnee **migrated** from the southwest sometime before A.D. 1600. They moved northward to present-day Nebraska and Kansas. They settled along the Loup, North Platte, and Republican Rivers.

Rolling hills of the Pawnee homelands

The Pawnee homelands had varied landscapes. In some areas, the land had lush native grasses that supported many types of wildlife. In other areas, stands of evergreen trees and forests of elm, ash, maple, and oak grew. The lands contained hills, canyons, and valleys. There were also rivers, streams, and lakes containing many types of fish.

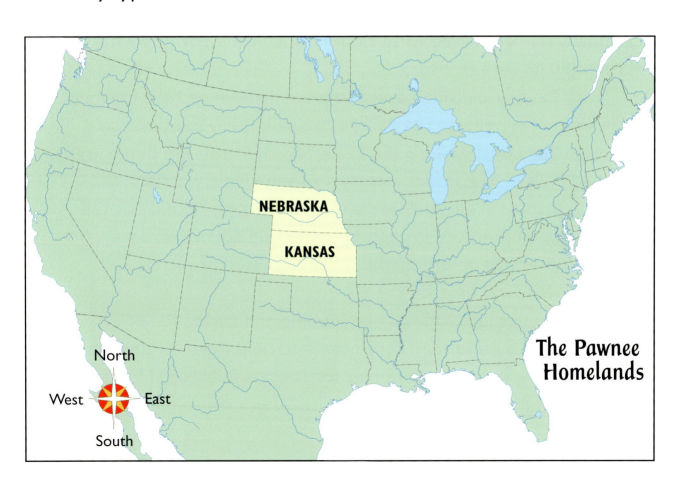

Society

    The Pawnee were divided into two political territories. The Skidi **band** lived to the north. The Chaui, Kitkihahki, and Petahauirata bands lived to the south. Each band governed and protected its own territory.

    Each band was divided into villages. The Pawnee built their villages in river valleys. The valleys contained rich soil that was excellent for farming.

    Each village had a chief, a council of sub-chiefs, warriors, and spiritual leaders. The chief was a respected man. He did not tell the people what to do. Instead, the chief and council leaders talked with the people. Together they discussed problems and decided what was best for the village.

    The Pawnee also had warrior, hunting, and curing societies. Some societies performed ceremonies to help them do their duties. Warriors held ceremonies for success in battle. Hunters' ceremonies ensured a good hunt.

Medicine people cured the sick. The medicine men and women also worked as spiritual advisers for the villagers. The medicine people received gifts in exchange for their services.

A Pawnee village

Food

    The Pawnee hunted, gathered, fished, and farmed. They grew corn, beans, squash, pumpkins, and sunflowers. Corn was their most important crop. The Pawnee believed corn was sacred. They performed a special ceremony at planting time.

    The Pawnee also ate fish. They caught crappie, perch, pike, catfish, bass, and trout in the lakes and rivers. The Pawnee caught these fish with stone hooks and handwoven nets.

    The Pawnee hunted beaver, rabbit, quail, turkey, prairie chicken, deer, and pronghorn. They also hunted American bison, which is often called buffalo. When the Pawnee went hunting, most villagers went to help with the hunt. But children, the elderly, and the sick often stayed behind.

    The Pawnee went on special hunting trips to follow the buffalo herds. The men hunted using bows and arrows, lances, and traps. Hunters approached the herd from downwind so the buffalo could not smell them. This allowed Pawnee hunters to get closer to the animals. Later, guns and horses made hunting easier.

Pawnee women preserved meat by cutting it into strips and drying the strips on racks. They mixed the dried meat with wild berries and buffalo fat to make pemmican (PEM-ih-kan). They stored the pemmican to eat while traveling. Women also dried fish to eat during the winter months.

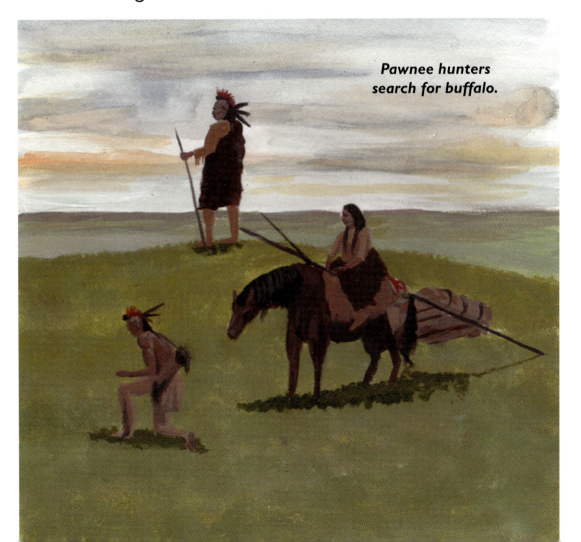

Pawnee hunters search for buffalo.

Homes

While hunting buffalo, the Pawnee lived in tipis. They easily moved the tipis using **travois**. Women set up and took down the tipis. Each tipi had a cone-shaped frame made of wooden poles. Women stretched buffalo-**hide** covers across the frames.

When not hunting buffalo, the Pawnee lived in earthen lodges. The lodges were partly underground. The Pawnee began building each lodge by digging a round pit about 25 to 60 feet (8 to 18 m) across. The sides of the pit formed the walls. Logs set into the ground formed a sturdy frame.

Next the builders covered the frame with smaller poles. Then they covered the frame and roof with earth. A hole in the center of the roof let smoke escape. Each lodge had a long, covered doorway. The door faced east to meet the rising sun.

Each lodge had an altar along the west wall. The people kept a sacred bundle and a buffalo skull on this altar. The sacred bundle contained items that protected the people. Women owned the bundle, but men used the items inside.

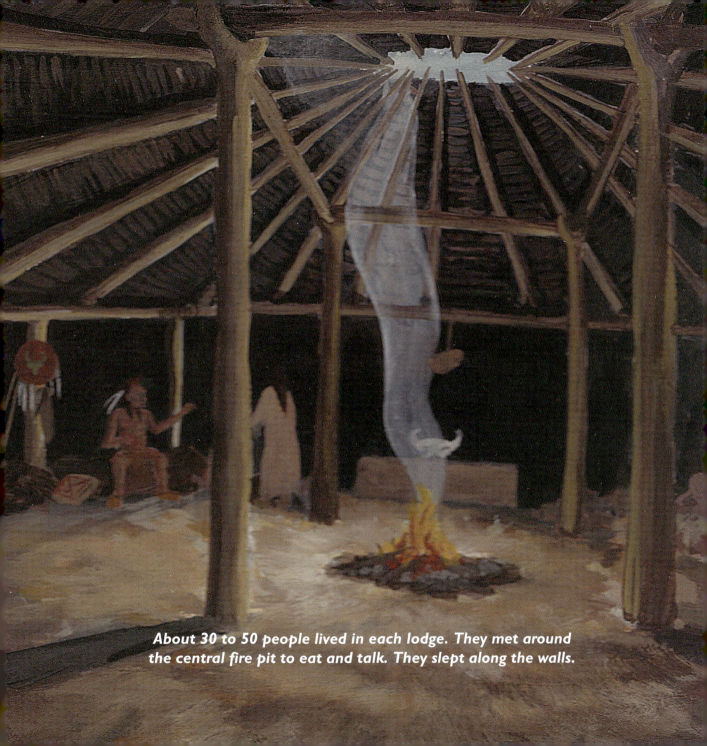

About 30 to 50 people lived in each lodge. They met around the central fire pit to eat and talk. They slept along the walls.

Clothing

    The Pawnee made clothing from deer, pronghorn, and buffalo **hides**. Men wore fringed, buckskin shirts. Women made each shirt by sewing together animal hides. Men also wore leather **breechcloths** and fringed, thigh-high **leggings**. The leggings protected their legs from brush and thorns.

    Pawnee women wore long, fringed dresses. To make each dress, the women often sewed together two deer hides. Women also wore wide belts decorated with **geometric** designs. Each woman's belt had a pouch for carrying tools.

    Women used **awls**, needles, and thread to sew and decorate clothing. They made sewing needles from the shin bones of deer. They used **sinew** for thread.

    The women decorated clothing with porcupine **quills**, animal teeth, and feathers. They also used dyes and paints made from plants and minerals. Later, after contact with Europeans, the Pawnee used glass beads, mirrors, and other trade goods.

In the winter, men and women kept warm by wearing robes made of buffalo **hide**. They wore moccasins on their feet.

Some Pawnee men shaved their heads except for a small piece of hair called a scalp lock. Then they rubbed buffalo fat and paint into the lock of hair. This made it stand up to look like a backward buffalo horn.

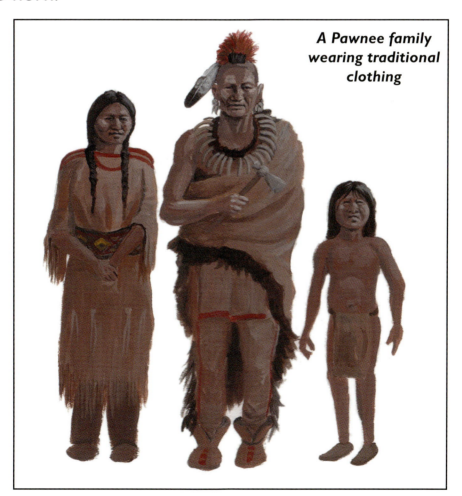

A Pawnee family wearing traditional clothing

Crafts

  Pawnee were excellent craftspeople. They made pottery and decorated clothing with paint and other materials.

  The Pawnee gathered clay from the riverbanks. Then they shaped the clay into pots. They used sharpened stone or bone tools to scrape designs around the edges of the pots. A traditional design was triangles filled with thin lines. They used the pottery for cooking, holding water, or storage.

  Pawnee women decorated their clothing with porcupine **quills**. The quills were hard. Women softened the quills by sucking on them. Once the quills were soft, the women sewed them onto clothing.

  Pawnee women used plants, berries, clay, and charcoal to make paints and dyes. They used the paints and dyes to color the quills and to decorate clothing in other ways.

  The Pawnee painted symbols on their horses to protect them from harm. They also painted pictures on buffalo robes to record their stories and history.

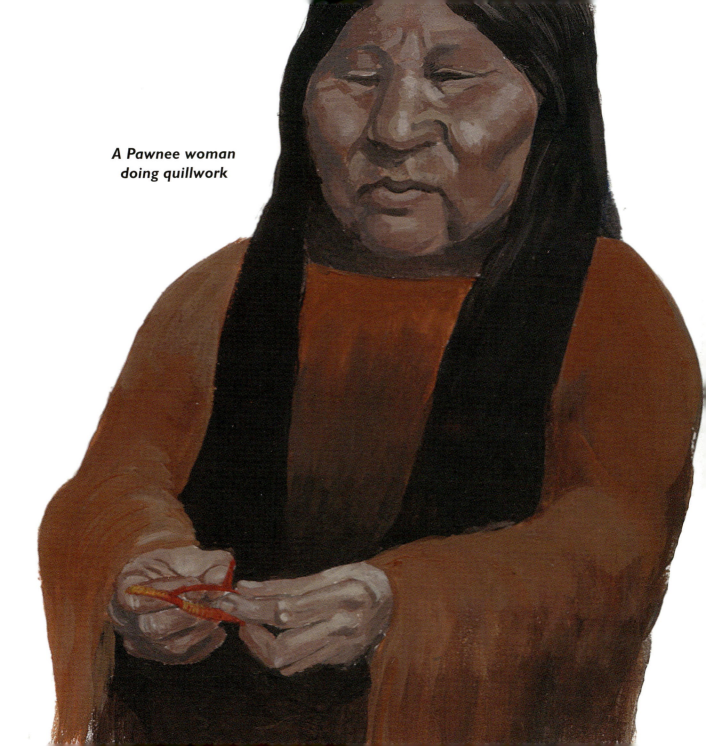

A Pawnee woman doing quillwork

Family

    The Pawnee in each village considered themselves one large family. They were very close and worked to feed and protect each other. Each person had a duty that was important to the survival of the Pawnee.

    About 30 to 50 people lived in each lodge. They divided each lodge into a northern and a southern section. Each section had a head of household. The sections were broken down into three stations.

    One station was for the middle-aged women. They did much of the work. Another station was for the young, single women who were learning their jobs. The last station held the elderly women. They cared for the children and took care of other jobs.

    The women cooked and prepared food for the winter. They made clothing and raised crops. Women prepared the buffalo meat and **hides**. They also set up and tore down the tipis when the Pawnee traveled.

When a Pawnee man married, he moved into his wife's lodge. Men hunted animals such as buffalo. They made weapons for hunting and protection. They also carved tools, spoons, and cups from buffalo horns and bones.

A Pawnee lodge

Children

    As babies, Pawnee children were carried on **cradleboards**. When the children grew older, they learned by helping their parents. Boys learned from the men how to hunt, fish, and make tools. They learned to make stone axes, arrowheads, and bows and arrows.

    Girls helped the women care for younger children. Young girls played with dolls made from leather. They made doll clothes and decorated them with **quill** or beadwork designs. This helped the girls learn how to take care of children and make clothing.

    The elders often told the children stories. The stories often taught the children lessons about life. But some stories were told for fun.

    The children played games that strengthened their bodies and minds. One game used a hoop made from an ash tree branch. The Pawnee wrapped leather around the hoop. They wove **sinew** inside the hoop like a spider's web. A small hole called the heart was left in the center of the web.

The children rolled the hoop or threw it in the air. Then they tried to throw a forked stick through the heart. Such games helped to sharpen their hunting skills.

Pawnee boys try to throw a stick though the heart of a webbed hoop.

Myths

The stars were an important part of the Pawnee's beliefs. They believed the stars created the Pawnee people.

A long time ago, before humans came, giants lived on Earth. The giants were very big. When they hunted, they hung freshly killed buffalo from their belts, the way young Pawnee hunters carry home rabbits.

The giants were destructive. They chased the animals and killed them for fun. They even spoke unkind words to the thunder and lightning spirits. This made the Great Spirit unhappy.

The Great Spirit unleashed thunder and lightning. He made it rain so hard that soon the Earth was covered with water. When the water dried up, the giants were gone.

Evening Star and his wife Morning Star gave birth to a baby girl. Sun and Moon gave birth to a baby boy. Whirlwinds gently carried the babies to the Earth. This is how the Pawnee people came to Earth.

A giant hangs buffalos on his belt.

War

Pawnee warriors had courage, endurance, and skill with horses. They often raided other tribes for horses. They left their villages on foot and quietly sneaked up on another tribe's camp. It was considered a great feat to return to camp riding captured horses.

In battle, the Pawnee used bows and arrows, knives, war clubs, and lances. For protection they carried shields made of the thick **hide** from a buffalo's shoulders. Men strengthened their shields by layering the hides.

Pawnee warriors wore breastplates made of long shell or bone tubes called hairpipe. The breastplates protected the men's bodies from arrows and lances. They also wore hairpipe chokers. The chokers protected their necks from arrows and knives.

Pawnee warriors did not always kill their enemies. Sometimes they earned honors by **counting coup** on an enemy. Riding close enough to an enemy to touch him with a stick, or taking an enemy's horse were deeds that took skill and courage.

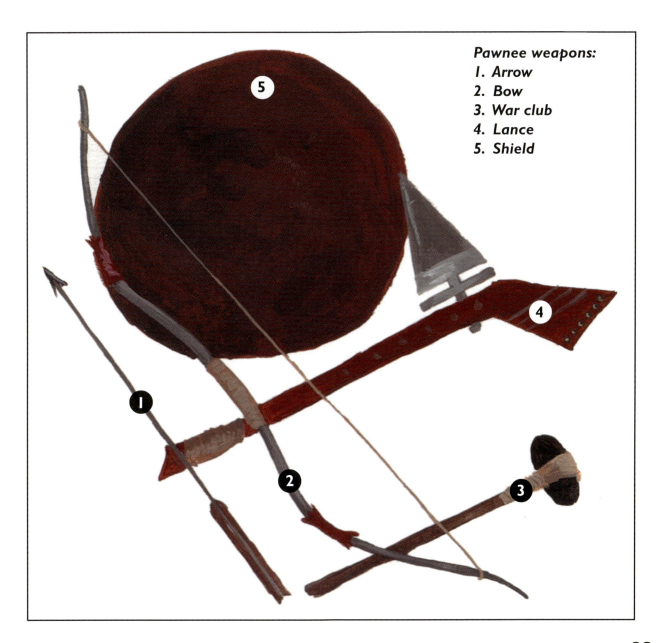

Contact with Europeans

In 1541, Francisco Vásquez de Coronado was the first European to meet the Pawnee. But other tribes lived between the Pawnee and European settlers. So the Pawnee did not meet other Europeans as early as many other tribes.

Spanish explorers brought horses to North America in the 1500s. By the late 1600s, horses had become a part of the Pawnee **culture**. Horses carried heavier loads than dogs. They also allowed the Pawnee to travel greater distances. This improved the Pawnee's ability to hunt, and to trade with European settlers.

In the early 1700s, the Pawnee began trading with French settlers in Louisiana. The Pawnee traded furs for glass beads, flour, blankets, mirrors, cloth, and guns. Guns helped the Pawnee protect themselves from neighboring tribes.

White settlers also brought diseases such as smallpox and cholera. Many Pawnee died. They did not have natural defenses against such diseases.

In the 1800s, some Pawnee warriors became scouts for the United States Army. The Pawnee Scouts helped the U.S. in campaigns against other plains tribes.

The Pawnee did not fight battles with the U.S. But they were still forced to give up much of their lands in Nebraska. The Pawnee gave up the last of their traditional lands in 1876. They were moved to a **reservation** in Oklahoma, and many still live there today.

Francisco Vásquez de Coronado meets with a Pawnee man.

Crooked Hand

Crooked Hand was a Pawnee chief of the Skidi **band**. He was born with a birth defect. His left hand was small and looked like a bird's claw. Although his hand was crooked, his birth defect did not stop him from becoming a fierce warrior and good leader.

Once, Crooked Hand had become sick and stayed behind while the rest of the village hunted. While the people were gone, the Pawnee's enemies attacked the village. Crooked Hand got out of his sickbed and gathered together the other sick men, the elderly, and the young children.

This group faced the invaders. It is said the Pawnee enemies laughed when they saw Crooked Hand's fighting force. But the Pawnee fought so fiercely that their enemies soon turned and fled.

Opposite page: Crooked Hand

The Pawnee Today

In the 1930s, the Pawnee Nation of Oklahoma developed a **constitution** and charter. They created the Pawnee Business Council and the Nasharo, or Chief's Council. These councils still govern the Pawnee Nation today.

Pawnee John Echohawk is executive director of the Native American Rights Fund. This organization fights for the rights of all Native American tribes.

In 1932, Chief William Riding In was a presidential elector for the Republican Party in Oklahoma. He was believed to be the only full-blooded Native American from west of the Mississippi River to be named for a political office.

In 1995, the fund helped the Pawnee win a case against the Smithsonian Museum. The museum returned the remains of 300 Pawnee ancestors, which had been on display. In June of 1995, the Pawnee reburied their ancestors' remains and burial objects in their traditional homelands in Nebraska.

Today, about 2,500 Pawnee are enrolled as members of the Pawnee Nation. Many of them live in the city Pawnee, in Pawnee County, Oklahoma. Other Pawnee live in other parts of the world. They all work at many types of jobs.

A young Pawnee man in a traditional costume (above and below)

The Pawnee have created language and **cultural** programs to preserve their ceremonies and traditional ways of life. Many Pawnee still gather together for celebrations such as the Pawnee Indian Homecoming and Powwow. During these social events, people celebrate their culture with ceremonies, singing, dancing, and games.

A.J. Leading Fox dances at a festival in Genoa, Nebraska, on September 1, 2001. About 50 members of the Pawnee Nation shared dress, dances, and songs with the community of Genoa.

Halla Rae Hawkins, 5, and her sister, Danielle Hawkins, 6, wait their turn to dance.

Glossary

awl - a pointed tool for marking or making small holes in materials such as leather or wood.
band - a number of persons acting together; a subgroup of a tribe.
breechcloth - a piece of hide or cloth, usually worn by men, that is wrapped between the legs and tied with a belt around the waist.
constitution - the basic laws of a nation or group.
counting coup - a military game where Native American warriors touched their enemies without killing them, then safely returned to camp.
cradleboard - a flat board used to hold a baby. It could be carried on the mother's back or hung from a tree so that the baby could see what was going on.
culture - the customs, arts, and tools of a nation or people at a certain time.
geometric - made up of straight lines, circles, and other simple shapes.
hide - an animal skin that is often thick and heavy.
leggings - coverings for the legs, usually made of cloth or leather.
migrate - to move from one place to settle in another.
quill - a stiff, sharp hair or spine.
reservation - a piece of land set aside by the government for Native Americans to live on.
sinew - a band of tough fibers that joins a muscle to a bone.
travois - a frame of two wooden poles tied together over the back of an animal and allowed to drag on the ground. It was used to transport loads.

Web Sites

The Pawnee Nation: **http://www.pawneenation.org**

Sheldon's Stories of Nebraska—The Pawnee
 http://www.ukans.edu/~kansite/hvn/books/nbstory/story28.html

These sites are subject to change. Go to your favorite search engine and type in Pawnee for more sites.

Index

A

animals 5, 8, 12, 14, 17, 20, 22, 24

B

bands 4, 6, 26

C

ceremonies 6, 8, 30
Chief's Council 28
children 8, 16, 18, 26
clothing 12, 13, 14, 18
Coronado, Francisco Vásquez de 24
counting coup 22
crafts 14
Crooked Hand 26

D

diseases 24

E

Echohawk, John 28
Europeans 12, 24
Evening Star 20

F

family 16, 17, 18
farming 6, 8, 16

fishing 8, 9, 18
food 8, 9, 16

G

games 18, 19, 30
Great Spirit 20

H

homelands 4, 5, 25, 29
homes 10, 16, 17
hunting 6, 8, 10, 18, 19, 24, 26

L

language 4, 30
lodges 10, 16, 17

M

Moon 20
Morning Star 20
myths 20

N

Native American Rights Fund 28, 29

P

Pawnee Business Council 28
Pawnee Nation of Oklahoma 28, 29
plants 5, 8, 12, 14

Q

quillwork 12, 14, 18

R

reservations 25

S

sacred bundle 10
society 6, 7
Sun 20

T

tipis 10, 16
tools 8, 9, 12, 14, 17, 18
trade 12, 24

U

United States 25

V

villages 6, 16

W

war 6, 22, 26
weapons 8, 17, 18, 22, 24

32